Seraphic Verses

The Lyrical Odyssey Beneath the Medlar Tree

SHINCE PETER MS

BookLeaf Publishing
India | USA | UK

Made with ❤ on the BookLeaf Publishing Platform
www.bookleafpub.in
www.bookleafpub.com

Dedication

Dedicated to my beloved children,

Evelyn Suzanne Peter and Elohim Issac Peter

The light of my life and the inspiration for every word I write.

May you always find your own voice, and may your hearts be filled with the same love

and wonder that you bring into my world every day.

This book is for you.

Acknowledgements

I offer my heartfelt gratitude to the Almighty for guiding my path with His boundless compassion and majestic grace, ensuring my actions were always under His watchful eye.

To my dear Parents, Sunny MP and Sholly Sunny, your unwavering love and patience have been the bedrock of my resolve. Your faith in me has been pivotal in my journey of endurance.

To Deepthi, Evelyn and Elohim, I am grateful for the moments of respite and laughter amidst the hard work. Your fellowship has been a wellspring of vigour and happiness.

A heartfelt note of appreciation to my friend Gayathri Ganesan for her artistic contribution in illustrating the cover of this book.

My friends deserve profound thanks for their steadfast support and the essential resources they provided, which were instrumental in bringing this endeavour to fruition.

Finally, I extend my acknowledgement to BookLeaf publishers for their assistance in bringing my collection of poems to the public eye.

Preface

Beneath the medlar tree, where time whispers and shadows play, 'Seraphic Verses' took root. This collection of poetry is more than just words on a page; it is a lyrical odyssey, a journey through the divine and the human. It was conceived in the quiet company of nature's own muse, where the rustling of leaves and the soft hum of the world around me provided the perfect backdrop for contemplation.

Each poem within this book is a fragment of my inner reverie, an offering to the beauty of the ineffable. Through these verses, I have sought to capture moments of grace and wonder, striving to touch the sacred in both the simple and the extraordinary. Here, words aim to weave the ordinary with the sublime, to uncover the divine in the world we often overlook.

Much like the medlar tree under which I wrote, these poems are a place of stillness, a sanctuary in the midst of life's hurried pace. They are a pause, a moment to reflect and to feel the deeper currents that move through us all. In this collection, I invite you, dear reader, to step into this shared reverie – to journey with me through the landscapes of the heart and soul, to explore the seraphic within and around us.

It is my hope that these verses may offer you, as they have offered me, a space of peace, beauty and quiet wonder.

In the spirit of shared wonder.
Shince Peter MS

Joyful Moments Beneath the Medlar Canopy

Above the window of my parents' room,
A medlar tree in winter's chill does bloom.
Its branches bear the promise of delight,
A fragrant herald in the silent night.

December's frost upon each leaf does kiss,
Yet warmth within our home will never miss.
For there, the medlar's scent does gently weave,
Through halls and hearts, on cold December's eve.

It whispers tales of seasons long ago,
Of family's love that in our hearts does glow.
Each petal's perfume, like a soft embrace,
Uniting kin in time's eternal grace.

The medlar tree, with blooms so rare and sweet,
Becomes the stage where past and present meet.
Its fragrance lingers in the joyful air,
A symbol of the love our family shares.

So every year, as winter skies turn grey,
The medlar's scent will guide us on our way.
To gather close, where love and laughter thrive,
Beneath the tree where family's love survives.

Celestial Calf: An Ode to Divine Pastures

In the meadow where the wildflowers sway,
A calf once danced, then quietly slipped away.
A friend to you, my child, so dear and small,
In your heart's pasture, it had a ball.

Its gentle eyes, a soft and soothing sight,
Now twinkle down from stars so crisp and bright.
Though tears may come and sadness for a while,
Remember its warm nuzzle, its playful style.

The calf now roams on heaven's endless farm,
Where fields are gold and no creature comes to
harm.
In dreams, it leaps, in joy forever cast,
A loving friend, whose memory will last.

So let your heart be light, my baby girl,
For love endures in life's swift, precious whirl.
Your calf, in fields of stars, finds peace and rest,
And in your thoughts, it's forever caressed.

Remember, love, though some may leave our side,
In hearts they stay, and in our souls abide.

Your calf, a petal in life's vast array,
In memory's garden, forever will stay

Harvest of Hopes: The Farmer’s Dream

In fields of green where paddies grow,
A gentle farmer, heart aglow.
With workers by his side, they sow,
Hopes for harvests that will overflow.

Their hands are rough, their spirits keen,
Together in the vast serene.
Each seed in earth, a silent vow,
For plentiful yields, they wish for now.

The farmer, with a tender glance,
Watches skies, gives crops a chance.
He prays for rain to grace their land,
For the sun to warm the soil and sand.

As stalks reach up to touch the sky,
Their hopes are lifted, spirits high.
The harvest’s gold rewards their care,
A bounteous yield, a farmer's prayer.

In unity with earth they stand,
A dream fulfilled by their own hand.
The gentle farmer knows the worth,
Of planting hope in fertile earth.

Echoes of Grace: The Village Bell's Blessing

Atop the hill, where whispers breeze,
Stands a church among the trees.
Its brass bell, aged with tales to tell,
Casts over the village a sacred spell.

With every toll, it sings of grace,
A sound that time cannot erase.
Its voice, a hymn of golden hue,
Bathes the village in blessings anew.

The bell's rich chime, so deep and bold,
Tells stories of the days of old.
It calls to hearts both young and old,
A unison of souls, a flock, a fold.

From dawn's first light to evening's close,
Its peal resounds; in it, love grows.
Each ring, a prayer that upward swells,
A benediction from the brass bell.

It weaves through alleys, fields and lanes,
A symphony that never wanes.
In every note, a promise dwells,

Of peace and hope, the brass bell tells.

The villagers, they feel its call,
A comfort blanket over all.
In every clang, a heaven's kiss,
A moment of communal bliss.

So let the brass bell's song extend,
From hilltop church to Earth's far end.
Its sound a gift that heaven sends,
A village blessed, a timeless friend.

Kindness Leads: The Gentle Teacher

In the heart of the classroom, where young minds
grow,
Stands a beacon of kindness, with a gentle glow. A
teacher with a smile, eyes warm and wise,
Sees each student's struggle, hears silent cries.

With chalk-stained fingers and a nurturing soul,
They plant seeds of knowledge, help dreams take
hold.
For every question asked, they have a patient ear,
Offering guidance and comfort, dissolving fear.

'Take your time', they whisper, 'it's okay to fall,
For in each mistake, there's a lesson for all'.
They weave through the desks, a calm, steady
force,
Steering young hearts with a compassionate
course.

Their words are like raindrops on a parched, dry
land,
Quenching the thirst for understanding with a
gentle hand.

‘Believe in yourself’, they say, ‘you have what it takes,
To climb every mountain, to cross every lake’.

In the quiet of the day, when the school's at rest,
The empathetic teacher reflects on their quest.
To nurture each spirit, to help them to see,
The power of empathy to set their minds free.

For knowledge is precious, but even more so is care,
In the hands of a teacher, who’s always there. With a heart full of empathy, they light the way, For the students they cherish every single day.

Small Deeds, Great Echoes

In the garden of life, where great oaks sway,
Not all can be the sun's bold ray.
But even the smallest seed, sown just right,
Can bloom with beauty, a pure delight.

Do small things in a great way, they say,
A kind word, a smile to light the day.
For in each act, no matter how slight,
Lies a spark of the infinite light.

The cup of water for a thirsty soul,
The helping hand to reach a goal.
A moment's patience in a line so long,
A simple tune hummed like a song.

These are the deeds that build the dome,
Of a world where kindness feels at home.
No need for fanfare, no loud parade,
In quiet grace, great paths are laid.

So let us cherish the little we do,
For small deeds form the morning dew.
And in each drop, the world's reflection,

Of simple acts and their pure perfection.

Remember, the stars that gently gleam,
Together cast the mightiest beam.
And so with us, our small things align,
To do them greatly and let them shine.

The August Ride

The August sun shines bright upon the
mountains.
Chilling wind and shining sun make me merry.
I am on a machine that carries my soul.
Four wheels carry the body, but two wheels carry
the soul.
From the rushes of town, I entered the pastures of
green.
Life is unpredictable, showing new paths in front
of us.
Wherever we think life ends, from there it starts
anew.
In this ride, thoughts direct you to your destiny.
You can ride the way you want.
The way will show your destiny, but we don't
know when we will reach it.
We don't know when our journey ends; ride
carefully, it's life.
Ride slowly; life is a journey, not a race.
When you ride fast, you forget where you are.
It will distress your ride, and you will forget
where you are going.
Love generously – nature, people, culture,
everything.

When you face obstacles on the path, be brave.
Now I know where I am riding; I am going to my destiny.
Destiny is not a matter of chance; it's a matter of choice.
On the path, I have seen my destiny; it's my death.
It's there to welcome me; let no one cry and weep.
Do not celebrate my funeral because,
When you are dead, you are dead – that's it!

The Business Planner for Life's Milestones

A grid of squares on the wall,
A silent guard, standing tall.
It marks the passage of our days,
In blocks of time, a temporal maze.

January's frost begins the tale,
A year anew, a fresh, blank slate.
February's love, a fleeting spell,
With March's winds, the seasons skate.

April showers bring forth May flowers,
A burst of life, a vibrant throng.
June then basks in rain's power,
While July's drizzle sings a sizzling song.

August lazes, sun-drenched days,
September's harvest, the bounty brings.
October's leaves in a fiery blaze,
November's chill, when winter sings.

December ends with festive cheer,
A cycle closed, the end draws near.
But time's a loop, a constant wheel,

The calendar, our fate to seal.

Each month a chapter, each day a line,
In life's great book, our stories twine.
The calendar, our guide and friend,
From year's bright start to its quiet end.

Mourning Innocence

In empty halls, I wander alone
Searching for a love that's no longer home
My mother's smile, a memory now past
A grief so deep, it forever will last

Her gentle hands that soothed my fears
Are gone, and I'm left with all these tears
I miss her voice, that whispered low
'I love you, child' as the winds would blow

In this vast world, I feel so small
Without my mother, I'm lost after all

I wish to turn back time, to hold her tight
To keep her close and make this endless night

But life moves on, though my heart stays still
I'll hold on to memories and cherish every thrill
My mother may be gone but in my heart
Her love will stay and never depart.

Rain's Surprise in the Desert

Beneath the dome of endless blue,
Where sun reigns with a fiery hue,
The desert sprawls, so vast, so still,
A canvas of the Earth's own will.

Yet, whispers of a change draw near,
As clouds above begin to peer,
And with them comes a rare delight,
A dance of rain against the light.

Each drop's a kiss upon the sands,
A fleeting touch by nature's hands.
They tap a rhythm, soft and clear,
A song the arid land holds dear.

The scent of rain on desert stone,
A fragrance only few have known.
It stirs the seeds that wait below,
To rise and in the brief wet, grow.

The rain may leave as quick as thought,
Its presence just a moment caught.
But in its wake, life finds a way,

A burst of green amidst the grey.

The desert knows this fleeting guest,
Will come and go at its behest.
Yet every drop's a treasured grain,
A moment's life, the desert's rain.

Learning Journey: The Scholar's Path

In silent halls, a scholar's quest,
With dreams and data, never rest.
Pages turn, the candles burn,
For truth and knowledge, they yearn.

Coffee sips and late nights blend,
On these, their waking hours depend.
Questions posed, in search of light,
Through study's maze, they fight the fight.

Posters hung, their findings share,
A global quest, a passion rare.
The thesis mounts, a peak to climb,
Each word a step, each thought a time.

At journey's end, a new path clear,
For research scholars, hold dear.
In labs and books, their minds take flight,
In pursuit of endless insight.

The thesis looms, a challenge to embrace,
Each argument put forth in its place.
The defence calls, a trial by peers,

A culmination of the years.

When victory's won, the scholar's heart takes flight,
A moment's pause, then back into the night.
For research is a journey, not a goal,
A scholar's life, the questing soul.

Red and White Carol Night

Beneath the velvet cloak of night,
A troupe of parish members, bright,
In festive red with caps of white,
Embark to spread the Christmas light.

Their voices rise in joyous song,
A melody that floats along,
The streets awake to their sweet throng,
As carols break the silent throng.

With lanterns glowing in their hands,
They traverse through the winter lands,
A chain of hearts in merry bands,
Uniting strangers, joining hands.

The Santa caps upon their brows,
Are crowns of cheer, to joy they vow.
In every lane and alley, now,
They bring the warmth of Christmas.

Their dresses dance like crimson flame,
A vibrant, living, moving frame.
With every note they claim,

The spirit of the season's name.

This carolling, a sacred art,
From soul to soul, from heart to heart.
In every word they do impart,
The love that Christmas charts.

So let the bells of Yuletide ring,
For parish members carolling.
In red and white, they come to bring,
The hymns of hope that angels sing.

Through Cracked Lenses

An old man looks through glasses cracked,
A village poor, his sight's impact.
His specs, all taped, a bit askew,
Show life's rich tapestry, old and new.

His eyes have seen many a year,
Through clear and broken glass, all dear.
A simple pair, his world to see,
Despite the cracks, he looks with glee.

Sunsets and smiles, through lines and breaks,
Each tiny shard, a story makes.
Though his view's not sharp or vast,
Through these specs, he holds life fast.

Children's laughter, a distant sound,
Through foggy lens, it still abounds.
His heart is full, his vision's not,
But in his world, he's not forgot.

An old man with his broken glass,
Sees more than many, in his class.
A villager, with little fame,
But through his specs, life's still a game.

Harvest of Sacrifice

In fields of gold, the eldest brother stood,
Working the land, doing all he could.
His father passed, left shoes too big to fill,
But he stepped in, with a strong, iron will.

He missed out on play, on school, on rest,
To make sure his family had the best.
While his brothers and sisters went to learn,
He ploughed the fields, for their future he'd earn.

No time for dreams; his own had to wait,
He worked through the sun, often so late.
He wanted his siblings to reach the sky,
So he gave his all, without a sigh.

He built their hopes from the earth and rain,
Never once did he complain.
He watched them grow and find their way,
Proud of the part he got to play.

Years flew by; his hair turned grey,
His strong back hunched, but still he'd stay.
His brothers and sisters, they flew so high,
Thanks to him, they got to try.

A quiet hero, without any fame,
He loved his land and played life's game.
For his family's love that was his flame,
In every seed, they'll find his name.

The eldest brother, who gave his youth,
For his family's future, that's the truth.
In the end, he saw the love he'd grown,
A farmer's gift, in love, it's shown.

Let's sing a song for the brother so brave,
Who gave so much, who gave all he has.
For his family's life, the path he paved,
The eldest brother, the love he saved.

Elephant in the Festival Light

In the land where the palm trees sway,
A festival dawns with the break of day.
The air is rich with the scent of spice,
And an elephant walks in a manner nice.
Adorned with gold, a caparison bright,
He moves with grace, a majestic sight.
His trunk held high, he greets the sun,
A herald of joy, the day's begun.
The temple doors open, the bells chime,
As he steps in rhythm, in time.
The people gather, a sea of faces,
Drawn to the spectacle, from all places.
Children laugh, their eyes wide with glee,
As the giant beast bows by the banyan tree.
He's a gentle giant, wise and old,
A part of the stories, long been told.
The drums beat a rhythm, fast and loud,
The elephant sways, proud in the crowd.
He's the star of the festival, the king of the day,
In the land of Kerala, where the good spirits stay.
His presence is a blessing, a touch of the divine,
As he walks through the temple, where the lamps shine.

The people offer prayers, and flowers too,
In the presence of the elephant, so grand and true.
For in this moment, there's no divide,
Between man and nature, side by side.
The elephant, a symbol of might and grace,
In the temple's embrace, finds his place.
So let's celebrate this wondrous sight,
An elephant in the temple, bathed in light.
For he brings together, with each step he takes,
The hearts of the people, for goodness' sake.

My Love, My Heart

In the soft wind, I hear a whisper, your name,
My love, a steady flame.
Your eyes, like stars in the night,
Shine with our love, so right.
Your touch warms me through and through,
A love so strong, so true.
In your arms, I find my rest,
With you, my love, I'm blessed.
Our love's a river, flowing free,
Through life's joys, just you and me.
We'll dance beneath the moon so bright,
Our love, a beacon in the night.
You're the song that my heart sings,
A simple tune with gentle wings.
With you, I want to spend my days,
My love, my life, in so many ways.
Hand in hand, we'll face what comes,
Our love, a beat like gentle drums.
Forever yours, in heart and soul,
With you, my love, I am whole.

The Timekeeper's Melody

In a quiet room, there stands a clock,
Old and crafted with hands that rock.
Back and forth, the pendulum swings,
Marking time with silent wings.
Its face shows hours that have slipped away,
With hands that move in a dance, night and day.
Numbers circle round, proud and fine,
Watching moments as they intertwine.
The pendulum cuts the air, back and forth,
Telling stories of the old earth.
It talks of days that are long gone,
In a tick-tock rhythm, it carries on.
Then comes the sound, so sweet and bold,
A ring that's like a story told.
It sings of time, hour by hour,
With a tune that has a gentle power.
Each ring spreads through the room so wide,
Telling time on every side.
It's a force that always stays true,
In the old clock with a swing, a view.
It holds secrets, and stories it shares,
Standing tall, it never wears.
In its ticking, we find a beat,
In the old clock with a swing, time's heartbeat.

The Ascent of Ambition

In the river's rush, a fish did swim,
Against the current, sleek and slim.
A waterfall ahead, so high and steep,
A challenge vast, a climb so deep.
Much like a soul with dreams in sight,
Striving for peaks with all their might.
The fish leaps up with all its heart,
Each splash a step, a work of art.
The water roars, a daunting sound,
Yet in its depths, a hope is found.
For every trial the fish endures,
A stronger fin, the climb assures.
So does the person, day by day,
Face life's falls in their own way.
With every setback, every fall,
They rise again, standing tall.

The fish, it dances with the flow,
Believing in the heights it'll go.
A leap of faith, a bond of trust,
In pursuit of dreams, it's a must.
And so the person, with eyes on the prize,
Through storms of doubt, will still arise.
For success, like the waterfall's crest,
Is but a journey, a relentless quest.

The fish may falter, may sometimes fail,
But with each try, it sets its sail.
And the person, too, learns from each no,
With every effort, they grow and glow.
At last, the summit, the fish will greet,
A triumph sweet, a feat complete.
The person, too, will find their place,
Atop life's falls, with grace and grace.
For both the fish and souls that strive,
It's the climb that makes them feel alive.
The waterfall, a symbol, a sign,
Of success earned, over time.

Nilambur: Home of Teak

In Kerala's warm hug, by the river's side,
Nilambur sits with quiet pride.
A green land full of teak trees tall,
Where nature's whispers to us call.
Old plots of teak stand firm and wide,
Telling stories of the past with pride.
These trees, like kings in their own right,
Stand strong and tall, a mighty sight.
The local tribes, with tales to share,
Live simple lives with little care.
Old homes with roofs that touch the sky,
Show off Nilambur's beauty, oh so high.
A museum there, all about teak,
Shares secrets of the forest, unique.
From tiny seeds to trees so grand,
It shows how teak has marked the land.
When the Rainforest Festival's in town,
Music and dance go round and round.
It's a time of joy for trees and folks,
With colourful art and nature's strokes.
Nilambur's charm is in every space,
A quiet, peaceful, natural place.
It's the air, the shade, the teak tree's power,
That makes this land a precious flower.
So come and walk through paths of green,

Chaliyar river's flow, so calm and clean.
Nilambur's arms are open wide,
In this teak town, we take great pride.

Echoes of a Father's Legacy

In the quiet of dawn, where whispers tread,
A son's heart heavy; his eyes are red.
A father's touch, now lost to time,
A debt unpaid, in silent chime.
He toiled in soil, in sweat and sun,
To raise a son, his only one.
Dreams he wove from dawn till set,
A future bright, no hint of debt.
But fate, unkind, with stealthy pace,
Stole the light from father's face.
Before the son could stand and earn,
Before the tides of life could turn.
The son, now draped in sorrow's veil,
Recalls the tales his father'd tell.
Of love and labour, hand in hand,
To sculpt a life, to till the land.

'I wish I could', the son would cry,
'To ease your pain before goodbye.
To give you rest, your toil to cease,
To offer you one moment's peace'.
But time's a thief, in shadows hides,
It waits for none; it splits no tides.

The son's regret, a burden deep,
In twilight hours, when others sleep.
He stands alone, amidst the stars,
Conversing with the moon and Mars.
'Forgive me, Father, for my lack,
For time I lost, I can't give back'.
Yet in the silence, love prevails,
A bond that through the dark sails.
For in each beat of the son's own heart,
The father's legacy, his art.
A promise made, beneath the sky,
The son's resolve, his aim to try.
To live a life that's full and just,
To honour him, in faith and trust.

A Verse of Restorative Empathy

In the garden of the heart, where compassion does bloom,
Restorative empathy, a light in the gloom.
A bridge over rifts, where understanding can grow,
A seed in the soul, in kindness we sow.
With gentle hands, we mend the fray,
Listening deeply to what others say.
In the mirror of minds, our reflections we see,
In the waters of empathy, we set grievances free.
A whisper of sorrow, a shared silent tear,
In the arms of forgiveness, we draw each other near.
Healing the wounds with the balm of our care,
In the tapestry of life, we repair each tear.
The chorus of humanity, in harmonious plea, Calls for a world where the heart is free.
Restorative empathy, the art of our time,
To understand, to console, in rhythm and rhyme.
For in the act of giving, we ourselves receive,
The grace of connection, in which we believe.
A dance of souls, in tender choreography,
Together we build a legacy of restorative empathy.

The Wealth of Tears

In the realm of wealth and worldly measure,
Where gold and gems are sought for pleasure,
There lies a liquid, priceless, rare,
Beyond the reach of market's glare.
Tears, the essence of our soul,
More precious than the purest gold.
A droplet born from joy or pain,
A treasure that we can't obtain.
In silence born, in shadows fall,
A tear reflects the heart's deep call.
A story told without a word,
The deepest voice that's ever heard.
It's not the salt, nor water's part,
But the silent language of the heart.
Each one a gem, unique, profound,
In tears, life's richest truths are found.
They speak of love that's lost, then found,
Of dreams that soar, then hit the ground.
A tear can whisper of regret,
Or memories we can't forget.
A single tear, a sea of emotion,
More vast than the deepest ocean.
A currency of purest form,
In joy and grief, in calm and storm.

So let us value each tear shed,
For in them, life's essence is spread.
The most expensive liquid, clear,
Is the silent falling of a tear.

Strangers' Grace: A New Town's Embrace

In a town where every face is new,
A traveller's heart seeks a clue,
To navigate the streets unknown,
One stands amidst the crowd, alone.
Yet kindness blooms in this strange place,
In the gentle smile on a stranger's face.
A guiding hand, a shared umbrella in rain,
Small acts of love easing the pain.
The currency of kindness, freely spent,
No expectation of repayment lent.
A meal shared on a bench in the park,
A light that guides one through the dark.
The map is drawn in acts of care,
From those who stop, who notice, who dare.
To reach across the void of 'unfamiliar',
To make a stranger's burden lighter to bear.
In this new town, where all is odd,
Kindness becomes the common thread.
Weaving through the streets like a song,
A melody to which we all belong.
For in the kindness of a stranger's eyes,
Lies the warmth of a thousand sunrises.
A reminder that no matter where we roam,

Humanity's touch can make anywhere home.
So here's to the strangers, now friends in my tale,
Who showed me that kindness will always prevail.
In a new town's embrace, I found my way,
Grateful for the kindness that strangers display.

The Paradox of Speed

He travels the fastest who travels alone,
No ties to bind, through the unknown.
A solitary figure against the sky,
Where horizons stretch and eagles fly.
No debate on which path to choose,
No time lost to another's muse.
With every step, he sets the pace,
In the silent solace of his own space.
The world unfolds at his command,
A fleeting kingdom, vast and grand.
No voice to question, no voice to stall,
He is the master of his all.
Yet in the quiet of his heart's recess,
Whispers of loneliness softly press.
For speed may win the race of time,
But shared moments make the climb sublime.
The laughter lost, the shared views missed,
The hand in hand, the goodbye kiss.
For speed and solitude may well contrive,
But in company, our hearts come alive.
So let him race against the sun,
And claim the victory swiftly won.
But know the truth that lies beneath:
We travel best when hearts entwreathe.
For though alone one may travel far,

It's love that shows us who we are.
The journey's joy, when all is done,
Is found in the many, not the one.

The Godliness of a Mother's Love

In the cradle of dawn, where life begins,
A mother's love, so pure, it spins.
A tapestry of warmth, a divine thread,
A reflection of God, where all is said.
She holds the universe in her embrace,
With every line of worry on her face,
A testament to her ceaseless care,
In her eyes, the depth of God's own stare.
Her hands, they shape the world with grace,
In every child, her features trace.
She teaches love without a single word,
In her echo, the voice of God is heard.
She forgives with a boundless sea,
Her heart, a shrine of clemency.
In her forgiveness, we understand,
The merciful touch of God's own hand.
Her strength, a fortress from above,
Enduring, relentless, like God's love.
Through storms and trials, she stands firm,
A testament to God's own term.
In every sacrifice, a silent plea,
A mirror of God's charity.
For in her giving, we receive,

A glimpse of God, we can believe.
So let us honour this earthly bond,
For in a mother's love, we find beyond.
A reflection of God, in human form,
In her embrace, all hearts are warmed.
For she is the vessel of life's great flood,
A mother's heart, the reflection of God.

First Step: The Dawn of Journeys

A journey of a thousand miles, it's said,
Begins with one step where we tread.
A single pace towards the distant goal,
A step of faith from the heart and soul.
Across the mountains, through the streams,
Past the valleys of our dreams.
Each step a story, a beat, a pulse,
In the grand symphony, a single convulse.
The road may wind, the path may bend,
But every mile will find its end.
For in each journey, no matter how vast,
It's the courage to start that will last.
With every sunrise, we see the way,
The journey unfolds day by day.
A mosaic made of trials and triumphs,
Of silent walks and noisy symphonies.
So take that step, though small it seems,
For it launches the ship of a thousand dreams.
The first footprint on a virgin trail,
The silent wish that fills the sail.
For the journey's heart is not the distance,
But the hope and strength in our persistence.
And with each step, we carve the track,

Of a thousand miles, there's no turning back.
So let us step with a steady pace,
For every journey has its grace.
And remember, as we travel through each mile,
It all starts with a single step and a smile.

The Triumph of Courage

In the shadowed corners of the mind,
Lurks a phantom, cruel and unkind.
It whispers doubts; it breathes despair,
The only thing we have to fear is fear.
It chains the spirit; it binds the heart,
Tearing all our dreams apart.
But within us lies a flame so bright,
A torch to hold against the night.
So let us face this ghostly foe,
With courage, we'll let our bravery show.
For fear itself is the only wall
That keeps us from standing tall.
We'll march ahead; we won't retreat,
In every challenge, we'll find fear's defeat.
For when we look it in the eye,
We'll see it's nothing but a lie.
The only thing we have to fear,
Is giving in to the whispers we hear.
So let's stand strong; let's stand as one,
Until the battle with fear is won.
For in the end, it's clear to see,
The shackles of fear, we hold the key.
And once unlocked, we're free to soar,
Beyond the fear, forevermore.

Stone of Hope

From the mountain of despair, so steep and tall,
Where shadows loom and darken all,
There lies a stone, not seen at first,
Amidst the rubble, quenching thirst.
A stone of hope, so small, so bright,
A beacon in the longest night.
It calls to those who've lost their way,
A promise of a brighter day.
For every mountain, craggy, vast,
Holds a stone of hope to cast
Into the waters of our fate,
To ripple out and navigate.
This stone of hope, a sturdy seed,
Planted in our deepest need.
It grows to break the mountain's might,
With roots of strength and leaves of light.
Out of despair, the stone is hewn,
A testament that change is soon.
It stands against the tide of sorrow,
A symbol of a new tomorrow.
So let us take this stone in hand,
And spread its hope across the land.
For out of despair, we all can cope,
With just one solid stone of hope.

Colours of Kindness: A Rainbow in the Cloud

In skies of grey, where shadows dwell,
And raindrops weave their sombre spell,
Be the light, the hue, the glow,
A rainbow in the cloud's low bellow.
Stretch across the stormy sky,
With colours bold, don't be shy.
A bridge of beauty, wide and tall,
A hopeful sign for one and all.
For those who wander in the mist,
Whose sunny days are sorely missed,
Your spectrum's arc, a tender vow,
To brighten moments here and now.
A whisper of the sun's embrace,
In the quiet of the rain's own grace.
You paint the world with joy's own sound,
When you become the rainbow in a cloud.

So let your colours boldly shine,
A testament of the divine.
For in each life, you can endow,
The light of love, right here, right now.
Be the peace that calms the storm,
The warmth that makes a heart transform.

For in your hues, you'll surely find,
The power to uplift mankind.
So rise above, be bold, be proud,
Try to be a rainbow in someone else's cloud.

Echoes of Grace

Every saint has a past, a tale untold,
Where shadows lingered and hearts grew cold.
In the alleys of sin, where the lost souls rove,
There walked a pilgrim, seeking light above.
A past of whispers, of tempests wild,
Where innocence slept, in the arms of a child.
Through the thorns of vice and the mist of despair,
A spirit wandered, in search of the fair.
The saint we revere, once danced with the night,
Embraced the moon's glow, shunned the dawn's light.
Yet in the abyss, where the stars feared to tread,
A seed of hope, in their hearts was spread.
With every misstep, a lesson was learned,
Through every fire, their resolve was burned.
From the ashes of past, a phoenix arose,
Adorned in virtue, shedding old woes.
A tapestry woven, from threads of the past,
In the loom of time, where nothing can last.
But the saint marches on, a beacon so bright,
Guiding lost souls, out of the night.
For every saint has a past, a story to tell,
Of climbing from depths, of escaping from hell.
And in their journey, we find our own way,
From the dusk of our past to the dawn of our day.

Crossroads of Light and Shadows

I began my journey down the desolate path,
Arriving at life's crossroads, I sensed an ominous wrath.
But hold your tears; don't heave a sigh,
This is not the end; my vision now spans wide and high.
Life's peculiar, with its unpredictable bends,
Don't lose heart when confronted with its trends.
Faith is perceiving light with the soul's sight,
Even when darkness veils your eyes with night.
Leave behind the pain that once took its toll,
Yet cherish the lessons that have enriched your soul.
Though the hurt feels deep and raw today,
In time, you'll see how it shaped your way.
With each step, let go of fear and doubt,
For growth and wisdom are what life's about.
In the tapestry of time, every thread has its place,
Every sorrow and joy, every fall and grace.
And as the horizon beckons with hues of hope,
Know that with change, you are equipped to cope.
For every ending is but a disguise,

A new beginning, a chance to rise.
So lift your gaze to the skies so vast,
The future awaits; the die is not yet cast.
With every dawn, life offers a new scene,
A chance to live, to love, to dream, to glean.

For better reasons, your life will have been rearranged,
Looking back, you'll appreciate how much you've changed.

Affection: The Milk of Love's Embrace

From the day I was born, I began to live,
My love for my mother, the greatest gift to give.
Without a shadow of doubt, clear and stark,
You are the one who taught me to walk.
You held me close when tears threatened to fall,
Guided my words, my first babble, my all.
With love's milk, you nourished my soul,
Shaping the person I am, making me whole.
Wherever I stand, whatever I become,
It's because of you, Mom, the nurturing one.
You are my steadfast tree, offering shade and rest,
The sunshine that brightens my life, making me blessed.
You are the hope that lights up my way,
The life within me, each and every day.
The strongest woman I've ever known,
In your love and strength, I have grown.
In your embrace, the world feels right,
A beacon of love, shining ever so bright.
Through every hardship, every tear and smile,
Your wisdom has carried me through every mile.
You're the roots that anchor me to the ground,
In your lessons of life, my faith is found.

With every sacrifice, you've sown a seed,
Of courage and kindness, to meet every need.
In the tapestry of life, you're the golden thread,
Weaving through my days, ahead I am led.
Your laughter is the music that fills my days,
A symphony of joy in so many ways.
To the world, you may be just one person,
But to me, you are the world; your love a constant sun.
For every moment, every breath, every frame,
I am grateful for you, Mom – forever the same.

Threads of Existence

Life, a journey, much like a ride,
With brakes that halt and hustle's stride.
At times it startles, at times it warms,
A blend of races, a dance of forms.
Stay vigilant, yet lose not your way,
In moments, let go, come what may.
Embrace the now; let sorrows wane,
For sunsets' grief may birth dawn's gain.
With each sunrise, a light bestowed,
Illuminates our path, our code.
Through love's deep plunge or disdain's drop,
By inspiration or sorrow's crop.
In life's grand play, whatever's penned,
Before the divine, as we ascend,
Proclaim with pride, without dismay,
'I've used my gifts, none thrown away'.
Each talent lent, I've stretched and spun,
Until the final setting sun.
With heart and soul, through every test,
I've lived, I've loved, I've done my best.

In life's rich tapestry, thread by thread,
We weave our stories, love and dread.
Through storms and calms, in light and shade,
Our choices craft the life we've made.

In every laugh, in each tear shed,
In silent whispers, words unsaid,
We find our strength, our will to fight,
To turn the darkness into light.
So let us journey, bold and free,
Embrace each moment's mystery.
For when we reach the final bend,
We'll find our purpose, meet our end.
With courage, kindness, hope and grace,
We'll leave a mark; we'll fill our space.
And in the end, our hearts content,
We'll know our lives were truly spent.

Steps to Renewal: A New Year's Journey

The calendar turns its final page,
Resounding in our thoughts, an ageless sage.
As the old year yields to the newborn's cries,
We dream, we weep, beneath the same skies.
Life's journey leads us through varied lands,
Let's release our sorrows, unclasp our hands.
Embrace the hope that the new year brings,
Behold – our future unfurls its wings.
With a drop of dew, fresh dreams we sow,
On the blank slate where ambitions grow.
A tome of days, each a virgin stage,
Inscribe your fervour, let passion rage.
With every heartbeat, etch your tale,
Promise that each moment shall prevail.
A voyage vast, a tale spun from dreams,
Begins with a step, or so it seems.
Let's add more lines to this life's verse,
With every triumph and every reverse.
May each chapter be written with care,
In the Book of Time, stories to share.
For every dawn, a new page to fill,
With laughter, love and a strong will.
Three hundred sixty-five chances anew,

To live, to learn and to start anew.
With courage, step into the unknown,
For in each seed of change, we have grown.
A journey of a thousand miles, indeed,
Starts with a single step – let that be our creed.

Guardian of Freedom

I walk a path distinct from the crowd,
Embracing deeds left unspoken aloud.
I battle what stands before my sight,
For the love of all I protect in the night.
It is I who champion your voice to rise,
It is I who guard the love under the skies.
It is I who ensure respect's gentle flow,
You ponder my name, but deep down, you know.
A warrior of valour, in courage, I'm clad,
A soldier am I, both solemn and glad.
I heed the call and march where I'm sent,
In the fields of conflict, my will won't relent.
A sentinel in the legion of the divine,
In God's vast army, steadfastly I shine.
I fight not for glory, nor for fame,
But for peace, for justice, in humanity's name.
Through the trials, through the thundering fray,
My spirit endures, come night or day.
For freedom's light, in the darkest hour,
I stand firm – a symbol of hope's unwavering power.

Rain's Embrace

Gazing out the pane, I saw the skies weep with grace,
Like a child in wonder, my gaze fixed in a silent embrace.
The heavens' tears wash over shingles and stones,
Sweeping away the needless, the world it atones.
With lids gently closed, my thoughts I confined,
Sensing the rain's caress, a peace within my mind.
Drops delve into my soul, a purifying art,
A silent plea to the divine, to purify my heart.
The gentle patter grows, a symphony of renewal,
Nature's tender rhythm, both tranquil and crucial.
Each droplet's touch, a whisper, a soft-spoken word,
A message from the ether, too profound to be heard.
I stand in quiet reflection, amidst the cleansing flood,
The rain, a mirror to my thoughts, now clear as the mud.
I ask of the celestial warden, with a hope so sublime,
To wash away my inner turmoil in this therapeutic clime.
The storm's tender mercy, a balm to the weary

soul,
In its nurturing embrace, I am once again whole.
As the clouds part ways and the sun begins to
shine,
I find a new beginning, in this heart of mine.

Ode to a Friend Forever

In the textile of life, a thread gleams pure and true,
A bond unyielding, a friendship ever new.
Through seasons of joy, through tides of tearful weather,
We walk the winding roads of this world together.
A friend forever, a beacon steadfast and bright,
Guiding through shadows, a star in the darkest night.
In laughter and in sorrow, in silence and in chatter,
What truly matters is us; nothing else does matter.
With hearts in tandem, our spirits soar and dive,
In the dance of existence, together we feel alive.
A promise unspoken, yet understood in our core,
To stand by each other, now and forevermore.
In the garden of companionship, our camaraderie blooms,
A rare flower of trust, defying life's glooms.
Rooted deep in the soils of mutual respect and care,
A friendship so resilient, a jewel beyond compare.
Through the ebb and flow of life's relentless quest,
In a friend forever, we find our haven of rest.

A mirror to our souls, in which our true selves reflect,
A kinship so profound, it commands the world's respect.
So here's to us, to the bond that time never severs,
To the laughter, the tears and the memories that tether.
A friend forever, a treasure without any measure,
In the story of our lives, the most cherished chapter.

The Majesty of Mother Nature

Mother Nature's gentle hands weave life's verdant quilt,
A mosaic of green and blue, on foundations of silt.
She breathes into the world, a symphony of existence,
Nurturing her creations with tender persistence.
Mountains stand as her sentinels, stoic and grand,
Guarding the secrets of her lush, fertile land.
Oceans echo her depth, vast and unexplored,
In their depths, the pulse of her heart is stored.
With each sunrise, she paints the sky anew,
In strokes of fiery hues, a dazzling view.
The sunset, her soft sigh, as day turns to night,
A canvas of twilight, until the morning light.
Forests are her sanctuaries, alive with her song,
A chorus of wildlife, where all life belongs.
Rivers, her veins, clear and life-giving,
Flowing to the beat of all things living.
She adorns the earth with flowers, a vibrant crown,
Petals of every colour, in meadows cast down.
Her breath, the wind, whispers through the trees,

A voice of wisdom, carried on the breeze.
In her embrace, we find our sustenance and home,
A reminder of the connection from which we've grown.
Mother Nature, our eternal guardian, so wild and free,
In her embrace, we find our unity, our destiny.
So let us honour her gifts, her boundless grace,
Preserve her beauty, her unparalleled embrace.
For in her health and vitality, our own lives are interwoven,
Mother Nature, our cherished guide, our haven.

The Quest for Freedom Regained

In the realm of ideals, where freedom's flag once soared,
Lies a silence profound, where once it roared.
The tapestries of liberty now tattered and frayed,
In the hush of the dawn, we find freedom mislaid.
Chains unseen bind the tongues that sang,
Of the rights and the truths for which the bell once rang.
In the marketplace of ideas, where discourse is trade,
Voices are stifled, and free thoughts fade.
The eagle that soared on winds of the brave,
Now watches, grounded, as a silent knave.
The torch that blazed a path so clear,
Flickers dimly, choked by the atmosphere of fear.
Where once stood sentinels, proud and bold,
Now lie whispers of the guardians of old.
The keys to the kingdom, rusted by neglect,
Unlock no more the rights we once held erect.
The pen, mightier than the sword, lies still,
Its ink dried up against the free mind's will.
The canvas of expression, once wide and unconfined,

Is narrowed, the colours of dissent confined.
In the shadow of statutes, the spirit wanes,
As the letter of the law, the soul's cry restrains.
The march of the free, now a muted parade,
A sombre reflection of the price that's been
paid.

Yet, within the quiet, a spark remains alight,
A flicker of hope in the encroaching night.
For freedom, once known, cannot be unlearned,
And the flame of liberty, once kindled, forever
burns.
So let us seek the paths once boldly laid,
To reclaim the freedom that has been mislaid.
With vigilant hearts and unwavering stride,
We'll lift the veil where true freedom resides.

A Girl and Her Water Lily

In a tranquil pond, under the sky so sunny,
A little girl with a water lily, as sweet as honey.
Her eyes, a mirror to the azure above,
Reflecting the innocence and the purity of love.
With gentle hands, she cradles the bloom,
Amidst the lilies, she's a living loom.
Weaving dreams in the daylight's embrace,
Her laughter ripples, a tender grace.
The lily, afloat on the water's chest,
Beside the girl, finds a place to rest.
Together they are, in silent rapport,
A scene of harmony, impossible to ignore.
Petals and dimples, both share a hue,
Of softest whites and a hint of dew.
Nature's child and her floral friend,
In this moment, their souls blend.
Oh, to be like the girl and the lily, so free,
Rooted in peace, yet floating with glee.
May we learn from this tender sight,
To live with love, and in light, delight.

A Father's Gift: Love Beyond Measure

In a humble room, with walls so bare,
A little boy waits with hope to spare.
His eyes, they gleam with innocent light,
For today's his day, his heart so bright.
The clock ticks on, the hours crawl,
A tiny ear listens for footsteps in the hall.
A cake, a gift, his wishes so small,
Yet in his world, they mean it all.
Outside the door, a figure stands worn,
A father's clothes, tattered and torn.
His hands, though empty, clench with might,
For he bears the weight of his son's delight.
The streets he roamed, from dawn till dusk,
His spirit unbroken, though life may be brusk.
Coins he gathered, few and spare,
To buy his boy the birthday fare.
With every step, his hope grew thin,
Yet giving up bore the greater sin.
A baker's smile, a deal struck kind,
A simple cake, with joy entwined.
A window's trinket caught his eye,
A toy, not new, but worth a try.
With bartered plea and heart so raw,

He claimed the prize with humble awe.
As twilight spread its purple hue,
The father's steps quickened, as if he flew.
A door creaked open, a boy's gaze met,
A moment etched, never to forget.
'Happy birthday, my son, my pride',
The father whispered, with love untried.
A cake, a gift, laid forth with care,
In a world so harsh, a moment rare.

The boy's eyes sparkled, a tear slid free,
For in his father's hands, he could see,
Not just a cake or a simple toy,
But a father's love, pure and coy.
So here's to the bond, both strong and deep,
To a father's promise, forever to keep.
For in the heart of a child so keen,
Lies the world's worth, in moments unseen.

Silent Words, Resounding Steps

In whispers tread through life's vast scene,
A gentle voice, a stance serene,
Yet in your grasp, a staff of might,
To guard your path, to lead what's right.
Speak softly; let your words be kind,
A soothing balm for every mind,
But let your stick, your silent creed,
Speak volumes when there's dire need.
Through forests dark and valleys wide,
With quiet steps, you'll be the guide,
The stick you carry, firm and strong,
Ensures your journey's safe and long.
The world may roar with noisy strife,
But calm you'll stay, throughout your life,
For with a stick that's big and sure,
You'll navigate through tempests' lure.
The stick's not just a tool of force,
But a symbol of a steady course,
A balance 'twixt the soft and hard,
A silent guardian, a watchful guard.
So carry on with whispered dreams,
And let your stick be more than it seems,
For in this blend of soft and far,
You'll find your strength, your guiding star.

Harvest of Despair

In the furrows where hope once grew,
Now lies a wasteland, a sombre view.
The river, once a friend so mild,
Turned traitor with a fury wild.
Its waters surged with relentless force,
A merciless, uncharted course.
My fields, my dreams, in its embrace,
Swept away without a trace.
The skies weep on, their tears unkind,
A mirror to the turmoil in my mind.
The land I tended with love and care,
Now a canvas of despair.
Gone are the sprouts, the green, the gold,
The future harvest I'll never hold.
The soil, enriched with toil and sweat,
Now a sodden, silent silhouette.
Where corn once danced to the sun's warm song,
The flood has silenced the vibrant throng.
The barn, the plough, all tools of trade,
In the mud, abandoned, they now fade.
The river's rage has ebbed away,
Leaving wreckage in its wake to stay.
I stand amidst the ruin, bereft,
Of hope, of heart, with nothing left.
The seasons turn, but I am lost,

A farmer with no seed to toss.
The flood has taken all I've known,
And I am left to grieve alone.
Yet in the depths of this dark night,
A flicker stirs, a spark of light.
For nature's hand that takes, restores,
And life, it seems, may yet have doors.

So I'll await the sun's return,
And maybe then the land will learn
To breathe, to bloom, to rise once more,
And hope will grow from sorrow's shore.

A Poem of God's Unfailing Love

In the valley of shadows, where light seems to wane,
Where the heart feels alone, embraced by its pain,
There, even there, in the depths of despair,
God's love is a fortress, His presence a prayer.
I am flawed; I am human, with burdens to bear,
Yet in my confession, I find He is there.
His angels, His messengers, sent from above,
To guide and to guard me in unconditional love.
Though I stumble and falter, and often I roam,
His grace is sufficient; it calls me back home.
For God's love is steadfast; it does not depend
On the worth of the sinner, but on being a friend.
A friend to the lost, to the broken in spirit,
He sees beyond failings, His love, can you hear it?
It whispers in breezes; it roars in the storm,
In the silence of night, His love is the norm.
Never to lose Him, that's the heart's silent plea,
For in His embrace is where I am free.
God's love is a beacon, a light that won't dim,
A reminder to all: we're never without Him.
So hold fast to faith; let hope be your guide,
For God's love is the river in which we all bide.

No matter the journey, no matter the strife,
God's love is the constant, the essence of life.

Timeless Chants of Orthodoxy

In the shadow of the ancient domes,
Where incense clouds the sacred rooms,
Orthodoxy, in her timeless grace,
Whispers prayers in a hallowed space.
Chanting echoes through the nave,
A song of faith the fathers gave,
Icons gazing from the walls,
Witness to the Spirit's calls.
Liturgies of gold and light,
Candles flickering through the night,
Mysteries held in every rite,
Guiding souls to heaven's height.
Apostolic lineage unbroken,
Sacred words for centuries spoken,
In the bread and wine, a token,
Of the love that Christ has woken.
Through the seasons of the soul,
Orthodoxy plays her role,
In the heart, she plants a goal,
Union with the Divine, the whole.
Tradition's stream, both deep and wide,
Where saints and martyrs have not shied,
To live the Gospel, crucified,

And in their living, they have died.
So stand within this ancient way,
Where orthodoxy holds her sway,
And find the truth that does not sway,
For in this faith, we kneel and pray.

The Forgotten Mango Tree

In the courtyard stands a mango tree,
Roots sunk deep, branches spread free.
A sentinel of time, a bearer of fruit,
Its leafy arms hold treasures, sweet and absolute.
Once upon a summer's generous blaze,
It offered up its bounty in golden days.
Children of the village, with laughter and cheer,
Gathered 'neath its shade, the mangoes near.
With sticky fingers and sun-kissed faces,
They climbed its limbs to the highest places.
A feast of joy, a memory made,
Under the mango tree's cooling shade.
Years have passed, the children grown,
To distant lands and lives of their own.
Riches they've found, in silver and gold,
Forgetting the tree and the memories of old.
Yet the mango tree, with patient grace,
Still stands in the courtyard, the very same place.
It blooms and it bears, as if to entice,
The return of the children, once fed by its vice.
The seasons cycle, the mangoes fall,
But the children, now adults, no longer call.
The tree remembers each name, each face,

Longing for the laughter, the joyous embrace.
A silent guardian of time's cruel tide,
The mango tree waits, with branches wide.
Hoping for a glimpse, a moment to share,
The sweetness of fruit, the warmth of care.
So if ever you wander, rich or in need,
Remember the mango tree's selfless deed.
For the heart of the courtyard, forever true,
Is the mango tree waiting, waiting for you.

Green Waves of Grain

In the green fields where rice begins,
A dance of earth and seeds that spin.
With hands that gently touch the ground,
To plant the seeds where life is found.
The farmer walks through water clear,
With young plants ready, he plants near.
Each one in mud, so soft and deep,
Where water and earth the seeds will keep.
The field's a mirror, sky so blue,
A peaceful place where rice will grow.
The plants they dance, a green sea wave,
They grow up strong; they grow up brave.
Day and night, the rice plants rise,
The farmer watches with wise eyes.
The plants get tall, with grains so fine,
A sign of food, a future sign.
The sun moves high, the rice turns gold,
It's time to harvest, time to hold.
The cutting starts, the rice falls down,
A rich reward, the farmer's crown.
The rice is freed from its tight shell,
The work is done, and done so well.
The rice is ready, from start to end,
A cycle done and will begin again.
Here's to the rice, from field to plate,

To farmers' work, both small and great.
For every grain, a story's there,
Of life, of land, of sky, of care.

The Red Cow

In the vale where the green grass grows,
A red cow lives, as the gentle breeze blows.
She's the pride of the family, their treasure so fine,
The source of their living, a bovine divine.
With udders so full, at the break of each dawn,
The farmer awakes, and with a stretch and a yawn,
He milks the red cow, her bounty to claim,
A pail full of milk, sweet as her name.
To the market he journeys, with milk fresh and pure,
Through winding paths and the morning's allure.
Villagers greet him, their coins they bestow,
For a taste of the milk from the cow they all know.
With pockets now jingling, his errands begin,
Buying groceries with care, a satisfied grin.
Bread, eggs and honey, some fruit for the bowl,
Each item he chooses to nourish the soul.
Back home he returns, where his family awaits,
With stories to tell and food for their plates.
The red cow looks on, her duty fulfilled,
In the circle of life, their bond is instilled.
So here's to the cow, the family's heart,
Together they thrive, never to part.
In the simple exchange of milk for their needs,
Lies a poem of life, where love intercedes.

Golden Grains and Evening Tunes

In fields of green, the gold does gleam, a sight so fair and bright,
The paddy roots spread all around, a farmer's pure delight.
With harvests high upon their heads, they walk with itself a steady pace,
The evening sun smiles warmly down, a golden, soft embrace.
The little birds, the sparrows chirp; they flit from here to there,
Pecking at the fallen rice, a feast they all can share.
The dragonflies in joyful flight; they zip and zoom with glee,
Beside the farmers, they do glide, as happy as can be.
This picture of the paddy fields, where work and beauty meet,
Reminds us of the simple joys, the cycle so complete.
For every grain that's gathered here, a story it does tell,
Of nature's gifts and human hands, that tend the

earth so well.
So here's a poem for the fields, the farmers and the sun,
For all the little creatures too, where life's web is spun.
In every stalk of paddy gold, there's a tale of peace and home,
A moment in the setting sun, a poem all its own.

Against the Tide

A fish swims upstream, through the rain's heavy pour,
To lay eggs, to give life, to the river's deep lore.
A human with dreams, in the world's vast expanse,
Strives hard, moves forward, gives their dream a chance.
Upstream, the fish fights, against the river's strong pull,
Each fin's mighty thrust, in the waters so cool.
A person with goals, against life's tough flow,
Keeps pushing, keeps dreaming, as they onwards go.
Rain falls, waters rise, but the fish won't relent, To the call of its future, it's fervently bent.
Humans, like fish, with their dreams held tight,
Face struggles and storms, but keep dreams in sight.

The fish and the dreamer, they share this same tale,
Through effort and will, they both must prevail.
For in life's heavy currents and the dreams we pursue,
It's the journey, the striving, that makes us anew.

Lotus Murmurs and Guppy Kisses

In a tranquil corner, where waters stand still,
A lotus pond nestles, by the old windowsill.
Guppy fishes dart, in a dance so divine,
Amongst pink petals, where sunbeams align.
Children's laughter rings in the gentle breeze,
As they play by the pond, with the greatest of ease.
Tiny hands splash, in the water so clear,
Their joyous echoes are a delight to hear.
The scent of the lotus, so fragrant and sweet,
Drifts through the air, in a perfumed retreat.
It flows to the home, with a whisper of peace,
As nature's own incense does never cease.
The blossoms unfold, with the dawn's first light,
A canvas of pink, against green leaves so bright.
The guppies, like jewels, in the daylight's embrace,
Add a sparkle to the water, and to the tranquil space.
Here, in this haven, where the heart finds rest,
The soul of the pond, is nature expressed.
A sanctuary of beauty, a symphony of bliss, Where lotus and laughter coexist in a kiss.
So let this poem be, a tribute to the scene,

A lotus pond at home, where life's simple and serene.
With guppies and flowers, and children at play,
The essence of joy, captured in words today.

First Steps to a Boundless Future

In the morning's tender light, by the schoolyard gate,
A mother's heart is heavy, her emotions in a state.
Tiny hands cling tightly, eyes awash with tears,
A symphony of childhood fears, the sum of all her years.
The little one, a mirror of the mother's soul,
With sobs that shake her tiny frame, a tolling bell's toll.
The air is thick with cries and wails, a chorus of despair,
As teachers, kind and patient, soothe the storm with care.
A mother's love, a sacred bond, now stretched a span apart,
The first goodbye, the hardest one, a test of every heart.
Yet through the tears, a vision clear, of futures bright and vast,
For education's golden key unlocks the doors of cast.
A baby girl, with ribbons tied amidst her golden hair,

Steps forward into learning's light, a journey they both share.
Though parting is a sorrow, sweet with bitter blend,
It's a step towards a future, where dreams and life extend.
So cry, dear child, and cry, dear mom, for this is love's own way,
A moment's pain for lifelong gain, as dawn turns into day.
For every tear that's shed today, a lesson's seed is sown,
And from these first, small, schooling steps, a mighty mind is grown.

Desert

My thoughts on a boundaryless world,
In that path half-covered by desert sand,
Beside the way, beneath the trees,
I saw some camels waiting for their final gasp.
The loyal ships of the desert, I decided to move ahead on the way,
Substantially declining the rational thoughts on sand grains.
When I reached my destination of human boundaries,
I saw the sandstorm dancing at its peak,
Nature at its best, vanishing the boundaries made by humans, compelling everyone to return from the spot.
My fear was for the camels; in this fragmentary journey, will they be alone in this desert?

God Made A Farmer

The Creator looked at His planned paradise and
decided He needed a caretaker,
Somebody who can wake up before dawn,
Who can milk cows, feed hens and ducks,
Somebody who can take care of a calf and goat,
Who can love his puppy like his own progeny,
Who can plant more saplings in his paradise,
One who can take care of his paddy and wheat
fields,
Somebody who can wait patiently for their
berries to ripen,
Who can forge the finest bond in his enclave,
The one who prays on his knees for rain,
One who cherishes his country, strong and who
feeds the entire world,
Who gets tougher as their lives keep getting
harder,
Who would giggle and then sigh, and respond
with pleased eyes,
When his son says he wants to spend his life doing
what dad does.
So God made a Farmer. Proud Son of a Farmer.

Corporate Buzz

In the towers of glass and beams of steel,
Where the corporate heartbeat throbs and feels,
A world of numbers, charts and deals,
Where time is gold, and silence heals.
Mornings rush with caffeinated streams,
As dreams are chased in PowerPoint dreams,
Desks align like soldiers in regimes,
In the glow of monitors' soft rays.
The clock ticks on, a relentless pace,
In cubicles, a confined space,
Ambitions race in an invisible chase,
Each face a story, each story a face.
Lunchtime chatter, a brief break,
From the endless quest to get it right,
A moment's peace in the daily fight,
Before the afternoon takes flight.
Emails flurry, meetings convene,
Decisions made, seldom seen,
A corporate dance, a well-oiled machine,
Spinning round, a routine unseen.
As dusk descends on cityscapes,
The office dims, escape takes shape,
Homeward bound, the workers gape,
At lives outside the corporate tape.
Yet in this hive of suits and ties,

Humanity and hope arise,
For within these walls, wisdom lies,
And the spirit of progress never dies.
So here's to those in the corporate mob,
Who find their place where they belong,
In the symphony of the city's song,
Together they move the world along.

Dreaming Dancer

In a quiet room, her ghungroos ring,
A story starts, with each step she brings.
Her eyes are talking, telling us more,
Her heart's secrets, start to pour.
Her feet tap out, a beat so sweet,
Telling tales, with every heartbeat.
The drums they match, her heart's own song,
Feelings dance out, where they belong.
Her skirt twirls round, in the air so high,
Showing her feelings, as she spins by.
Her hands move through, telling her tale,
In the dance, her voice doesn't fail.
Each hand sign lets her feelings fly,
A girl's dreams, reaching for the sky.
Kathak dance, her way to share,
What's in her heart, with flair and care.
In the light, her story's clear,
A dance of hope and sometimes fear.
The girl and dance, together they say,
Her silent words, in a moving play.
So here's to the dance, that captures the soul,
In its whirlwind of stories, making us whole.
Kathak, the dance, a timeless embrace,
A poetic journey through movement and grace.

Special Memories

In my heart, memories dance, light and warm,
Treasured times, too deep for words to form.
Though miles stretch wide, you're never far,
In my heart's home, you're a bright, constant star.
You've been my rock when paths grew steep,
In quiet office corners, memories we keep.

Your encouragement shone, led me through,
Now I miss the buzz, our shared view.
Side by side, we faced each day's quest,
Caring, sharing, striving for our best.
Though now apart, a brief pause in our song, Life's
twists and turns can't hold us for long.
I trust in better days, with your support so sure,
Hope is our anchor, steadfast and pure.
On this dark night, let's wait for morning's light,
Holding on to hope, to make our spirits bright.

Elohim, My Shining Star

In the realm of dreams, you were born to shine
Elohim, my son, a precious gift divine
Your name, a reflection of the divine above
A blessing to our family, a labour of love

Your smile illuminates the darkest of nights
A beacon of hope, that shines with delight
Your laughter echoes a joyous, contagious sound
A treasure to behold, a heart that's pure and found

As you grow and flourish, may your spirit soar
May your heart remain kind, and your soul forever more
May you walk in wisdom, and may your path be bright
Elohim, my son, my love for you will be your guiding light

In your eyes, I see a future bright and bold
A young man with a heart that's brave and made of gold
I promise to be here, to guide and support you along
Elohim, my son, my love for you will forever be strong.

A Bad Day's Shadow

Dark clouds gather, and the skies grow grey
A bad day's shadow, follows me all day
Every step I take, feels like a chore
The world outside seems, to be a dull roar

The morning sun, that once shone bright
Now hides behind, a veil of endless night
The coffee's bitter taste, the traffic's maddening pace
Everything conspires, to ruin this day's space

But still I hold on, to a glimmer of hope
A chance that tomorrow will bring a brand-new scope
A fresh start awaits, like a blank page so white
A bad day's shadow, will fade into the night

So I'll take a deep breath, and let the day unfold
And though it's been tough, I'll find a way to be bold
For every bad day, has an end in sight
And tomorrow's sunshine, will bring new light.

Whispers of Home: A Heart's Journey

In distant lands, I roam and stray,
But my heart remains, in a different way.
For in my home, where love does abide,
My heart finds solace, and a peaceful tide.

The river's gentle flow, that surrounds my farm,
Echoes whisper, of a love that does no harm.
The fish that swim, in its crystal clear stream,
Seem to await my return, with a silent dream.

My garden's vibrant hues, that bloom with every season,
Yearn for my footsteps, and a gentle reason.
My pets, that faithful crew, who stand by my side,
Wait for my return, with a loving, longing stride.

The trees that shade, the wind that whispers low,
All seem to whisper, 'Come back home, and let your heart glow'.

So I'll roam no more, but hasten to my nest,
Where love and peace await, and my heart can find its rest.

For home is where the heart is, and mine is there, it's true,
With the river, the garden and the love that shines through.

Two Friends, A Cosmic Debate

Two friends sat under starry skies,
Discussing life's great mysteries and sighs.
'Heaven and hell', they pondered with care,
'Do they exist, or are they just myths we share'?

One friend spoke of ancient tales and lore,
Of gods and goddesses, and the heavens' score.
The other countered with reason and might,
'Perhaps it's just a concept, a guiding light'.

They delved into the depths of human desire,
The quest for answers, the burning fire.
They wondered what lay beyond the grave,
And if the afterlife was a reward or a wave.

As the night wore on, and the stars shone bright,
They came to a realisation, a newfound sight.
'Heaven and hell', they said with a grin,
'Are not some distant place, but right here within'.

'We create our own heaven, our own hell on
Earth,
Through the choices we make, and the love we

give birth.
So let us spread kindness, and live with glee,
And create our own heaven, right here, wild and free'.

With that, they stood up, and looked up at the sky,
Feeling the universe's vastness, and the beauty that lies.
They smiled at each other, and hugged with delight,
Knowing that heaven and hell are just a choice, a beacon of light.

Journey Through the Whispering Woods

In the heart of the woods, where whispers begin,
My vehicle treads paths, where light grows dim.
A drizzle descends, a soft evening's embrace,
While the fading day paints the sky with grace.
Through the canopy, a reddish glow is cast,
On leaves of light yellow-green, contrasts vast.
Deers dart and dance, in playful, gentle trots,
Nibbling roadside grass in tranquil spots.
The peacock's call, a melody profound,
Echoes through the trees, a haunting sound.
Birds streak the sky, to their nests they soar,
Nature's creatures, all heading to their door.
Alone I drive, through the forest deep,
The moon above, its vigil does keep.
Its silver light, a companion so bright,
Guiding me home, through the encroaching night.
It seems to sigh, a lunar lament,
For my solitary journey, time spent.
Yet in its glow, I find a silent friend,
Whose light whispers, 'I'll be with you to the end'.
The forest around, a protective shroud,
Guarding my way, silent yet proud.
Every tree, every leaf, in silent decree,

Ensures my passage home, safe as can be.
This journey alone, a path I must tread,
But with the moon and the woods, I'm gently led.
To the warmth of home, where my heart does
yearn,
Beneath the stars, until the sun's return.

Eternal Ambition

In the heart of time's vast sea,
Where moments are waves, fleeting and free,
I cast my eye beyond the horizon's creed,
For I desire nothing less than eternity.
Not a whisper of greed in this solemn plea,
But a yearning for the infinite embroidery.
A wish to weave through ages' thread,
Where past and future are seamlessly wed.
I stand firm in belief, unshaken, unbowed,
In the face of the temporary, I am not scared.
For what is life but a temporary lease?
In the quest for forever, I find my peace.
The universe echoes with timeless tales,
Of stars and spirits, of cosmic scales,
And in this grand design, I seek my part,
A perpetual symphony, a never-ending art.
So let the world call it a dream too steep,
I'll hold my conviction, vast and deep.
For in the pursuit of eternity's embrace,
I find the truest expression of grace.
Time's river flows; to no end it yields,
Through unseen valleys, o'er uncharted fields.
My spirit sails on, with hope as its mast,
Bound for the shores of the boundless and vast.
Simple is the heart that beats with this quest,

To live beyond time, in eternal rest.
A dreamer, perhaps, but with vision clear,
Chasing the forever, year after year.

Through the Lens of Higher Consciousness

Before you set a label's weight upon a soul,
Pause and ponder on the unseen toll.
For beneath the surface, silent battles rage,
Stories untold, hidden on life's vast stage.
They may be sailing through the fiercest storm,
Bearing scars unseen, far from the norm.
So tread gently, let your heart be your guide,
Offer a harbour where secrets can confide.
Be kind to others, for kindness is a balm,
A soothing whisper in the night, a calming psalm.
It's the light that pierces through the darkest night,
A beacon of hope, an embrace that holds tight.
Seek to understand, before you judge what you see,
For perspectives shift, and what is, may not always be.
Listen with intent, not just with your ears,
But with a soul that sees beyond the years.
Analyse the world through a lens so clear,
Where higher consciousness draws near.
It's a vision that sees beyond the mere facade,
To the essence of being, the soul unflawed.

In this dance of life, where roles constantly shift,
Let empathy be your gift, and spirits uplift.
For when we view each other with eyes kind and wise,
We find our humanity, and together we rise.
Remember, the world is a reflection of our collective gaze,
So let's look with love, and set the skies ablaze.
With the light of understanding, compassion and grace,
We'll build a world where every heart finds its place.

A Tale of Feather and Hearts

In tempest's tearful torrents, a sparrow's plight,
A nest once cradled high, now lost to sight.
Amidst the thunder's roar and wind's cruel jest,
A feathered heart beats wild in a tiny chest.
It cries for mother's warmth, for beak's soft touch,
For sheltering wings that mean so very much.
The rain, relentless, mocks its desperate plea,
A symphony of sorrow, wild and free.
Parallel in pain, a man roams the street,
His mind a maze, where past and present meet.
Once held a love, so tender and so true,
Now wanders lost, in skies no longer blue.
His heart, a nest uprooted by life's storm,
In search of solace, a place to feel warm.
The love he knew, a memory's embrace,
A haunting echo in time's vast, cold space.
Both the sparrow and man, their fates entwined,
In search of something precious, left behind.
One longs for mother's call, one for love's trace,
Both victims of a cruel, unyielding chase.
Yet in their cries, a silent hope does dwell,
For broken wings and hearts can surely heal.
With time's soft hand to mend the deepest scar,

They'll find their way, beneath the evening star.
So let the rain pour down, let the thunder roll,
For in the storm's eye lies the searching soul.
And there, in quiet moments in between,
The sparrow's nest and man's lost love are seen.
A tale of loss, of longing and of pain,
A sparrow's cry, a man's love sought in vain.
Yet in their journey, a truth we ascertain:
In loss we find the love we seek to regain.

A Grandmother's Reflection

In the heart of winter's chill,
Leaves do fall, and time stands still.
Round the fire, the children close,
Grandma's stories, softly compose.
Woollen caps and sweaters tight,
Fingers warm in firelight.
Distant church bell's solemn ring,
Melodies of memories sing.
Years have passed, the room's grown bare,
Grandma sits in her fireside chair.
The laughter's gone, the warmth has fled,
With grown-up dreams, the children spread.
Alone, she watches embers' glow,
Recalling faces, all aglow.
The fire crackles, breaks the hush,
In her heart, a longing rush.
She sees them there, in the flame's dance,
In every spark, a second chance.
The bell still tolls; it's far away,
A call to those who could not stay.
With every flicker, hope's reborn,
For grandkids' return, she sits forlorn.
By the fire, she waits each day,

For time to bring them back her way.
A simple tale of love's strong tie,
Of parting ways, of time gone by.
In winter's grasp, she holds them near,
In every flame, they reappear.

Cherished Moments on Christmas Eve

In a home where time ticked by,
A father's work piled to the sky.
On Christmas Eve, a night so clear,
His little girl approached with cheer.

'Where are the stars'? her small voice peeped,
'The crib, the tree'? her eyes, they wept.
Her tiny heart, with hope deferred,
Longed for the joy of festive word.

The father paused, his papers strewn,
Felt life's swift pace, a silent tune.
Those precious moments, oh so rare,
A chance to show his heartfelt care.

He rose with purpose, set aside
The endless tasks, his worldly pride.
From dusty boxes, memories flow,
Old paper stars began to glow.

With hands that worked through many nights,
He hung the stars, the blinking lights.
Each ornament, with care, was placed,

Upon the tree, in perfect taste.

The crib was set, each figure right,
Little Jesus in the soft moonlight.
His home transformed into heaven's part,
A canvas of his own heart's art.

The little one, with joy so grand,
Leapt and danced, a merry band.
Her laughter filled the silent space,
A symphony of love's embrace.

The father watched, a tear escaped,
As childhood memories took their shape.
The Christmases of yesteryears,
Now echoed through the joyous cheers.

In that small room, the world stood still,
Love wrapped around the winter's chill.
For in the end, it's love we keep,
On Christmas Eve, when angels peep.

Together there, in festive light,
A family's heart took flight that night.
For Christmas is a time to give,
And in those moments, truly live.

Evening's Gentle Symphony

Beneath the evening's amber light,
The sun dips low, yet still so bright.
Birds chart their course through painted skies,
Homeward bound, their day's work lies.
The bustling streets with people filled,
Their labour done, their roles fulfilled.
The church bell tolls its solemn song,
Calling hearts where prayers belong.
In kitchens warm, the mothers toil,
Preparing feasts from the soil.
Aromas waft through open space,
A prelude to the meal's embrace.
Outside, the laughter of the young,
Their school day's end, their freedom sprung.
Games of joy in twilight's glow,
Innocence in the world they show.

The waterlily, graceful, poised,
Folds its bud with nary a noise.
A silent herald for the night,
Welcoming the moon's soft light.
As dusk descends, the world's embrace,
A tranquil scene, a gentle grace.

In every corner, life's sweet tune,
Under the watch of the rising moon.

Echoes of the Unwritten: A Poet's Lament

In the mind of the poet, a silent plea,
For words that once flowed, now lost at sea.
A quill lies idle; ink has run dry,
Pages stay blank, no matter how hard he may try.
He wanders through streets, in search of a muse,
In every corner, for clues he peruse.
The clatter of life, the whisper of trees,
He listens for rhythms carried by the breeze.
The world unfolds in a tapestry wide,
Yet the poet's heart is locked from inside.
A tumult of thoughts, a maelstrom within,
Seeking a spark, for creation to begin.
He gazes at stars, in the velvet night,
Hoping for verses to take their flight.
The moon's gentle glow, the silence of space,
Still, the words elude, vanish without trace.
In cafes, he sits, watching life's dance,
Each sip of coffee, like a second chance.
Conversations swirl, laughter rings clear,
But the poem he seeks, never draws near.
He climbs the mountains, breathes the air so thin,
To find the voice that echoes deep within.
The peaks stand proud, under heaven's dome,

Yet the words he craves, refuse to come home.
The poet's soul, a battlefield of doubt,
Where once was certainty, now there's drought.
A yearning for beauty, to capture in rhyme,
But time ticks on, unforgiving, sublime.
In the quiet of night, he confronts his fear,
The terror that his muse may never reappear.
A silent prayer, to break through the block,
To once again feel the key turn in the lock.
The struggle is real, the path unsure,
But the love of the craft, forever pure.
For even in darkness, the poet knows deep,
The words will return, from their hidden sleep.

An Onam Day Ode

Onam's dawn breaks with a gentle hum,
Children gather, their fingers deftly come,
To lay a carpet, blooms of every hue,
A floral tapestry, morning kissed with dew.
Gents in kurtha, shirts of pristine white,
Ladies draped in sarees, a traditional sight,
Kerala's grace in threads of cream and gold,
A tale of culture and heritage, centuries old.
The air is rich with scents of Sadhya feast,
Banana leaves with dishes, not in the least,
A spread of flavours, twenty-one or more,
A culinary journey, right at your door.
Children laugh, their spirits taking flight,
On swings that arc into the sunlit bright,
Back and forth, their joyous cries ring clear,
In celebration of a time they hold dear.

Awaiting Mahabali, the king of yore,
His return from the nether, as lore,
To see his land in prosperity's embrace,
And bless his people, a smile on his face.
Onam, a festival of harvest and cheer,
Where unity and happiness appear,
In every corner of this verdant land,
Together in heart, together we stand.

So let the Pookalam reflect our dreams,
And Sadhya bond us in communal streams,
As we don the attire of our ancient ways,
We celebrate Onam, in heartfelt praise.

The Family Man's Quest

In the heart of the city's relentless hum,
A man sits, his spirit weary and numb.
His hands, once eager, now idly rest,
Upon a desk that's become his nest.
Each keystroke a chain, each call a shackle,
In the corporate sea, he's but a mere tackle.
Dreams of azure skies and lands afar,
Trapped behind his monotonous bar.
He yearns for the mountains, the rivers, the breeze,
The rustling leaves, the towering trees.
To wander the earth without bounds or end,
To every beckoning horizon, he'd wend.
But at home, there are mouths to feed,
Little ones with dreams and need.
Their laughter, their future, in his hands lie,
For them, he puts his own dreams aside.
His passion for travel, a silent ember,
A flame he must remember, yet not surrender.
For in their eyes, he sees a different journey,
One of love, hope and life's attorney.
So he stays, in the grind, day by day,
A sacrifice, in love's name, he'll pay.
But in his heart, the wanderlust whispers,
'Perhaps, one day', as hope gently flickers.

9 789367 393741

Printed by Libri Plureos GmbH in Hamburg, Germany